CONTENTS

Emma: End Titles

Music by Rachel Portman

Arranged by Richard Harris

FABER ff MUSIC

The text paper used in this publication is a virgin fibre product that is manufactured in the UK to ISO 14001 standards.
The wood fibre used is only sourced from managed forests using sustainable forestry principles. This paper is 100% recyclable.

First published in 2009 by Faber Music Ltd
Bloomsbury House 74–77 Great Russell Street London WC1B 3DA
Cover by Lydia Merrills-Ashcroft

Music processed by MusicSet 2000
Printed in England by Caligraving Ltd

ISBN10: 0-571-53322-1
EAN13: 978-0-571-53322-0

25
29
33
37
41
45
rall.

Pride and Prejudice: Main Theme

Music by Carl Davis

17
mf
21
25
R. H. over
f
29
33
p
36
fp
mf warmly

40
44
48
p
sub. f
f
52
55
fp
poco a poco cresc.

59
mf
mf warmly
62
66
mf
70
L. H.
ff non legato
73
fp
L. H.
p sub.

Persuasion: Main Theme

Music by Jeremy Sams

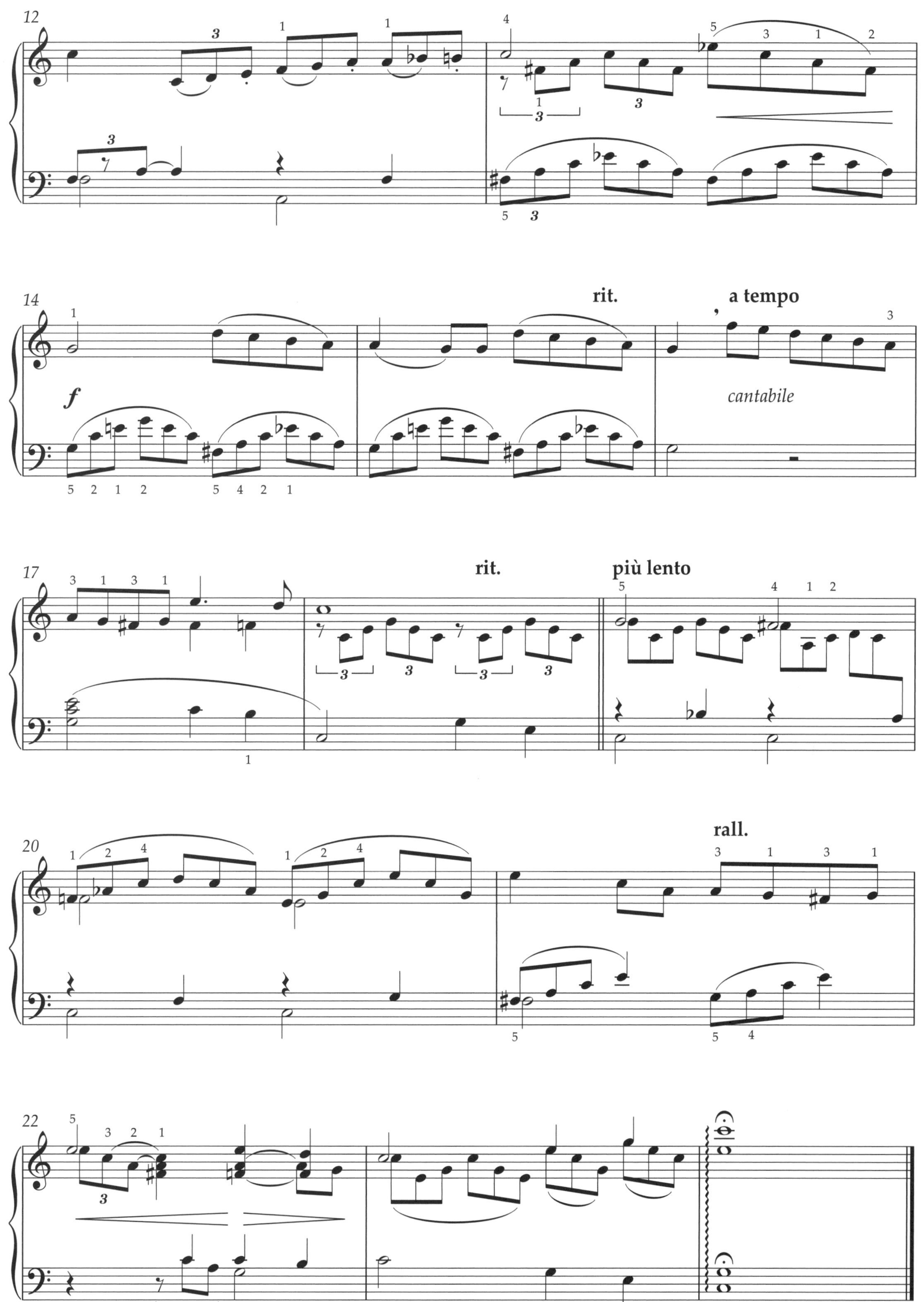
12
13
14
f
rit.
a tempo
cantabile
17
rit.
più lento
20
rall.
22

Pride and Prejudice: Andante Favori WoO 57 (excerpt)

Music by Ludwig van Beethoven

24
cresc.
p
28
cresc.
sf
p
32
36
cresc.
sf
p
40

43
cresc.
46
49
dolce
54
cresc.
cresc.
59

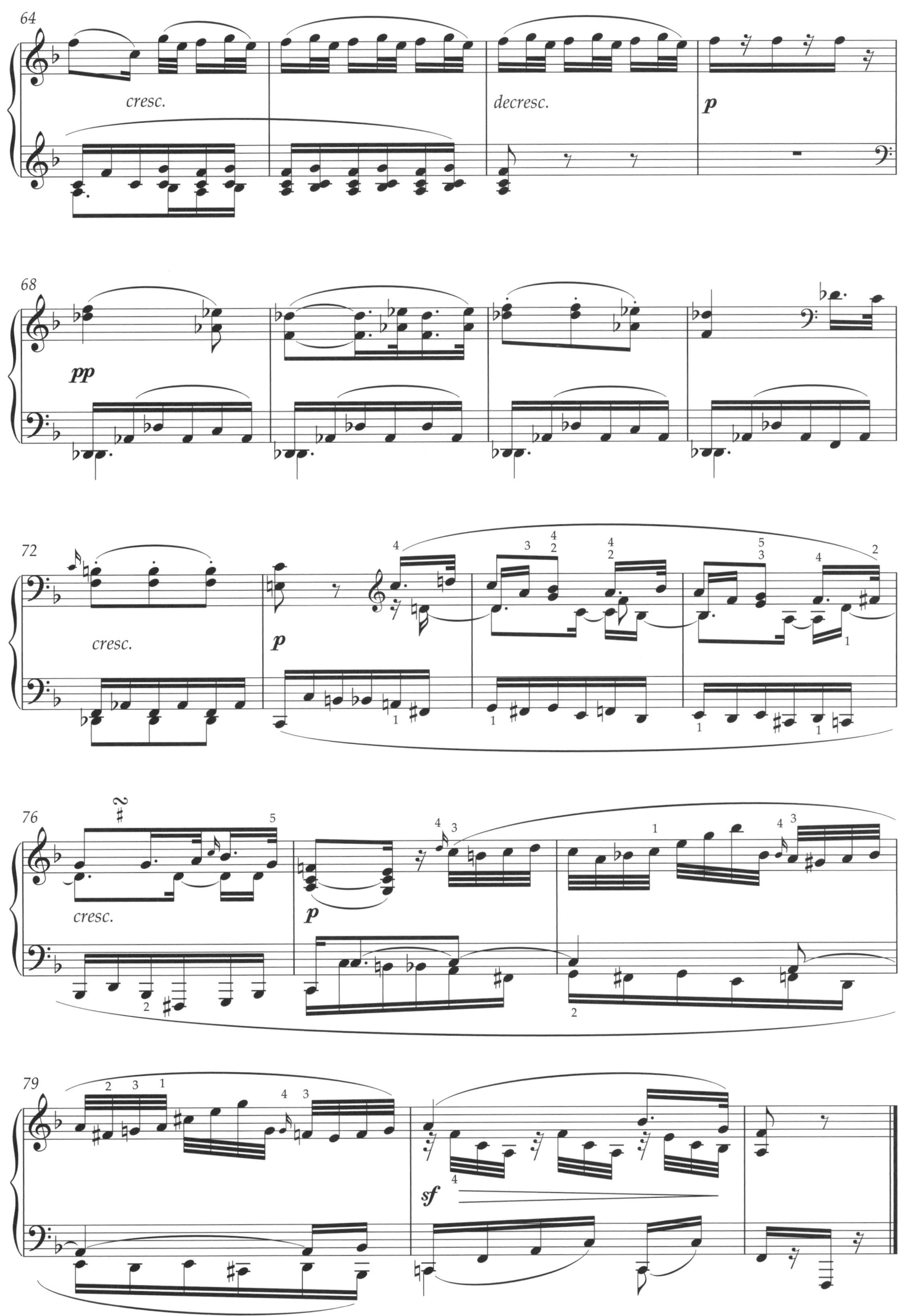
64
cresc.
decresc.
p
68
pp
72
cresc.
p
76
cresc.
p
79
sf

The Mayor of Casterbridge: Main Theme

Music by Carl Davis

18
p
22
R. H.
25
pp
28
pp
32
mf
pp

Tempo I
p
mf
mf
p
slightly broader
f

Pride and Prejudice: Andante from Sonatina Op. 36, No. 4

Music by Muzio Clementi

Cranford: Main Theme

Music by Carl Davis

24
p
29
34
p
39
mf
mp
43
p
mp

48
mf
53
mp
58
63
68
72
rubato
p

Becoming Jane: An Adoring Heart

Music by Adrian Johnston

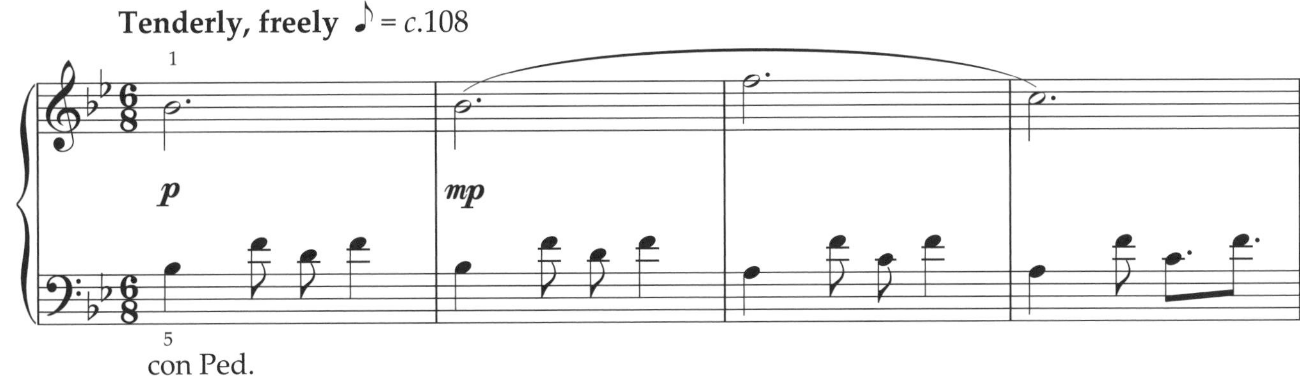

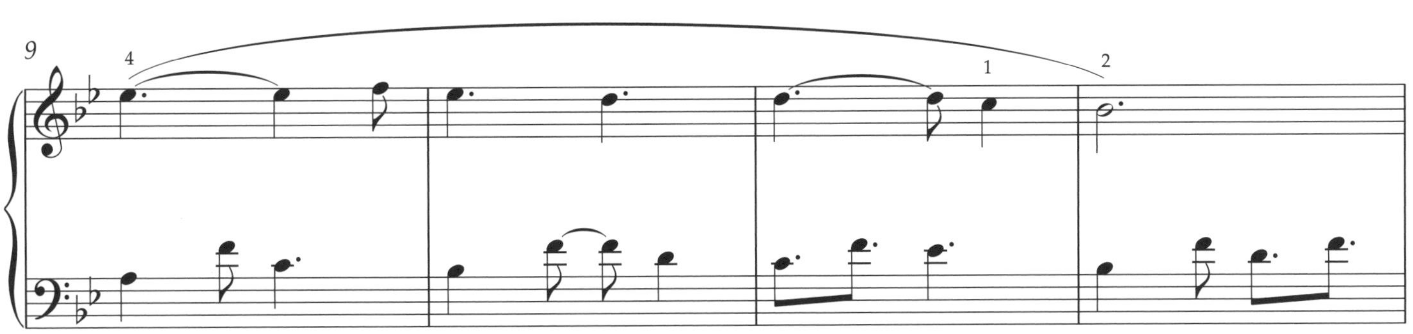

Pride and Prejudice: Rondo alla Turca from Sonata No. 11 in A major, K331

Music by Wolfgang Amadeus Mozart

65
p
70
76
82
f
p
tr
89
f
92
1

CODA
2
97
4 3 1
102
107
p
112
117
f
123

Brideshead Revisited: Sebastian

Music by Adrian Johnston

25
29
p
mp
8
34
(8)
p sempre legato
39
44
mp
P
sim.
49

54
mf
59
5
64
poco rit.
a tempo
1 2 4
1
mf
mp
mf
69
8
f
73
mp sempre legato
77
rit.
p

Shakespeare in Love: The Beginning of the Partnership

Music by Stephen Warbeck

mf
f
mp
f

45
49
mp
mf
53
57
mp
61
p
mp

A Passage to India: Main Theme

Music by Maurice Jarre

poco rit.
a tempo
Slower ♩ = c.72

Middlemarch: Main Theme

Music by Stanley Myers

21
mp
25
mf
mp
30
mf
p
35
mf
p
mf
p
40
mp

Howard's End: Return to Howard's End

Music by Richard Robbins

17
mp
P
21
p
pp
p
L.H.
P
26
L.H.
P
8
30
(8)
mp
p

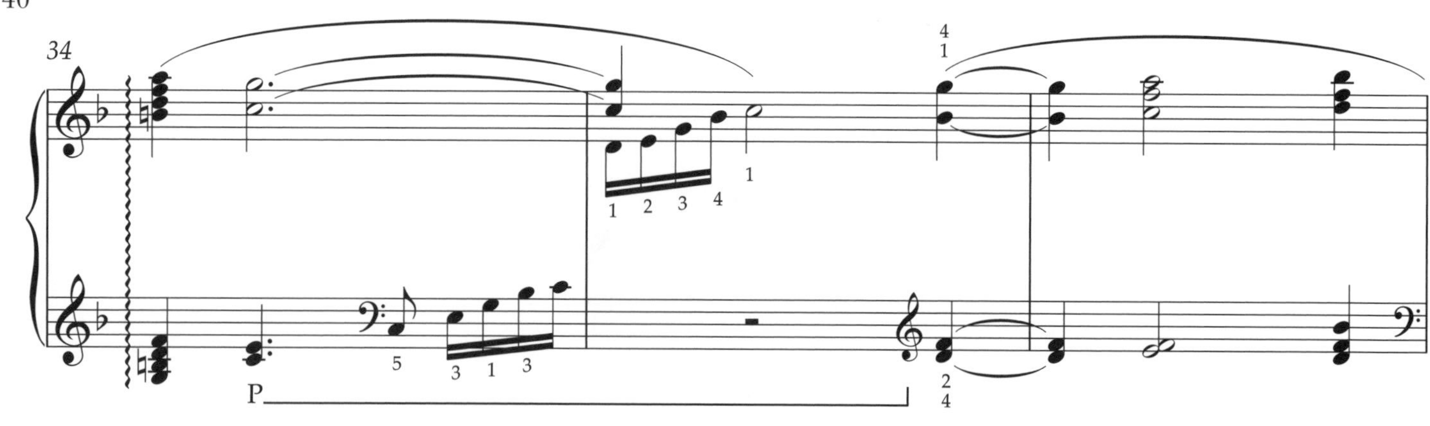
34
P

37
P
P

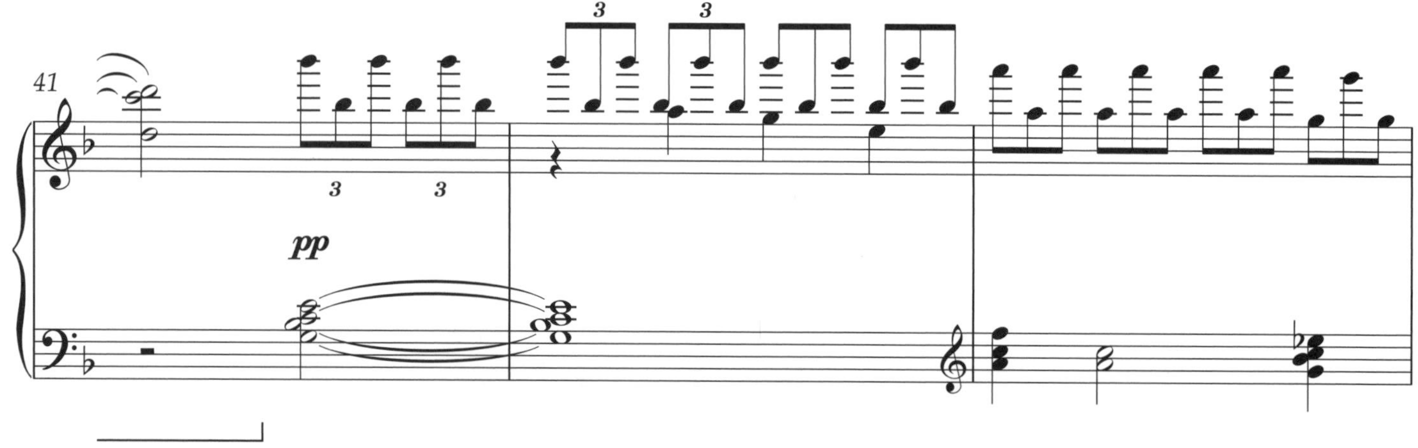
41
pp

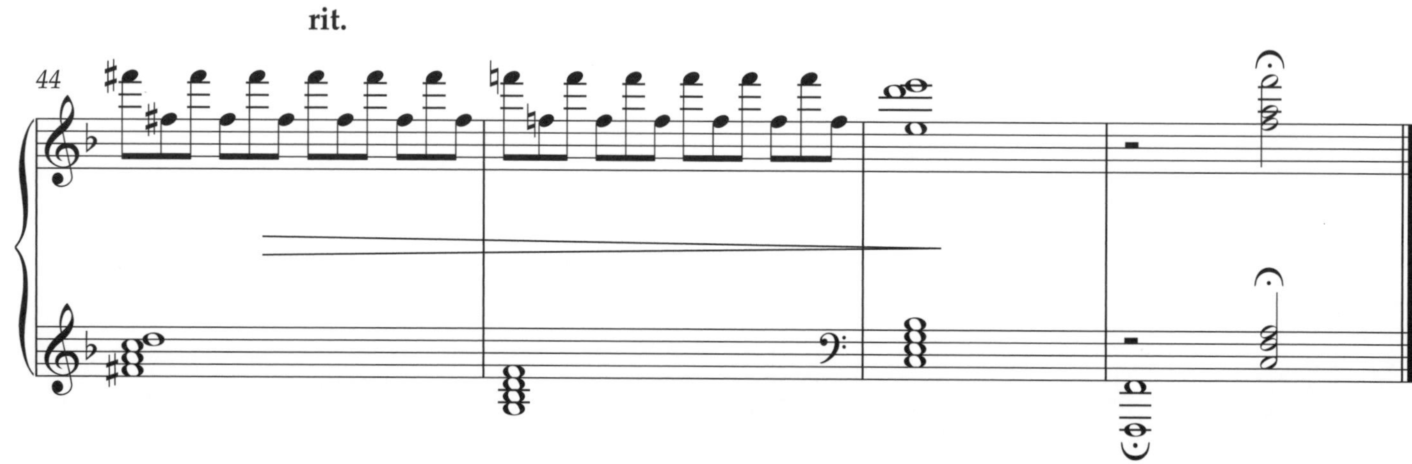
rit.
44